ISBN Print: 978-1-998651-89-4

Dedicated to Amy

OSTRICH

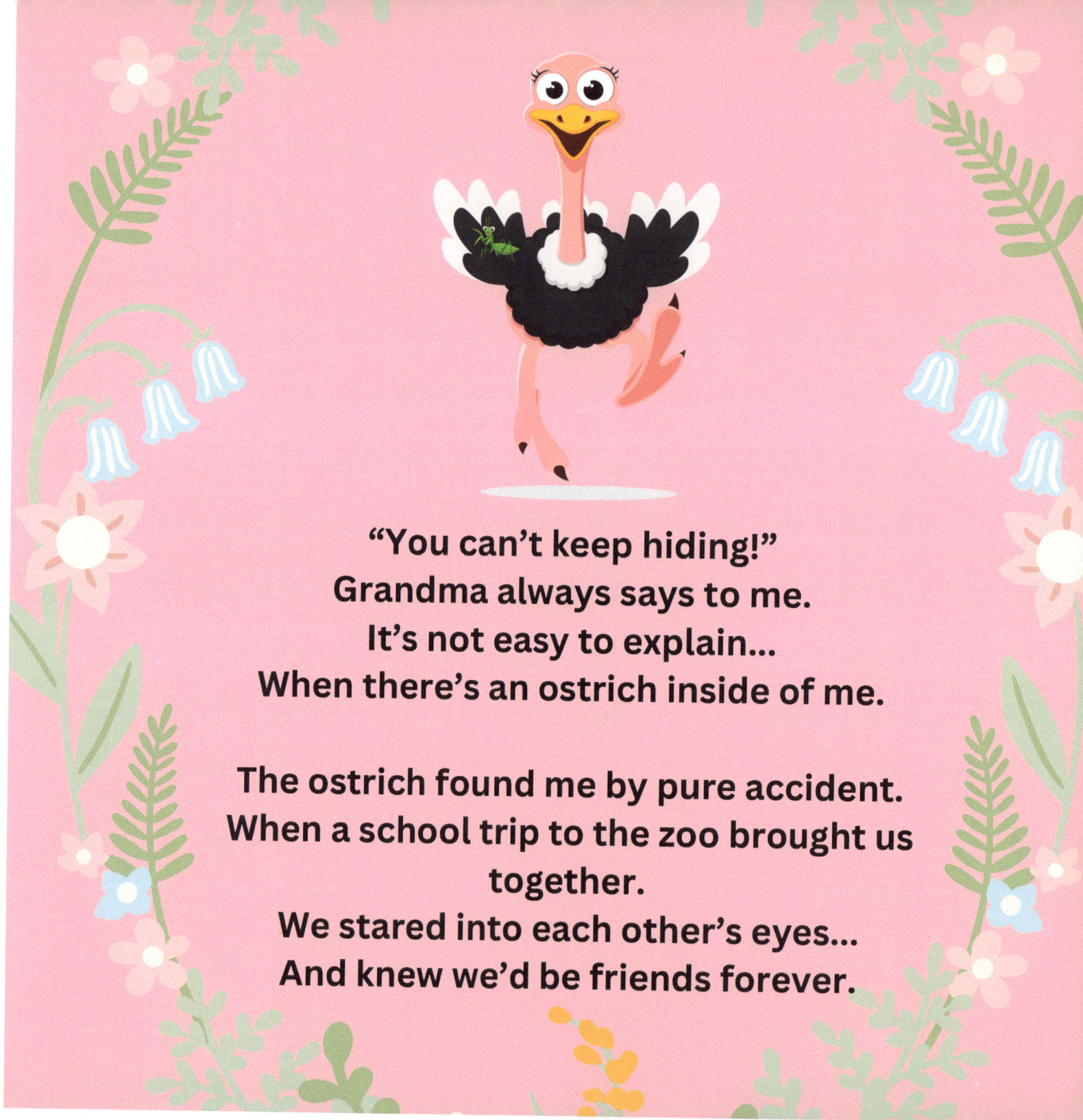

"You can't keep hiding!"
Grandma always says to me.
It's not easy to explain...
When there's an ostrich inside of me.

The ostrich found me by pure accident.
When a school trip to the zoo brought us
together.
We stared into each other's eyes...
And knew we'd be friends forever.

Neither of us make friends easily...
There was a connection between us immediately...
So now we hide our heads in the sand side by side.
My ostrich BFF and me.

WOMBAT

I don't know why...
There's a wombat inside of me.
I don't know anything about wombats...
And they don't know anything about me!

HUMMINGBIRD

I used to love to sing...
Until a hummingbird flew inside of me.
Now whenever she hums I hum too..
And I flutter wings which are imaginary.

Humming is easier - no words to remember.
All I do is put my lips together and hum.
My humming doesn't make a beautiful song...
But it sure cheers me up when I feel glum!

SHADOW

Trip and fall. Dance big not small!
There's a shadow following me...
He isn't like a normal shadow...
Because he lives inside of me.

He comes out of his shell...
Every day, 24/7...every place I go!
Even indoors, in the classroom...
He steps out and takes a bow!

WIND

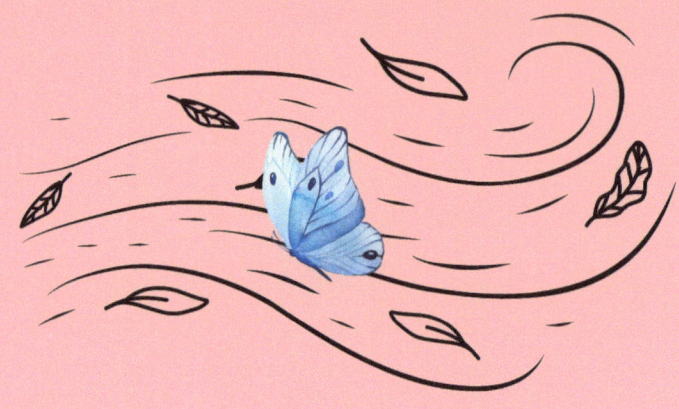

The wind calls my name...
Whenever I feel lonely.
She offers me company...
The wind lives and breathes inside of me.

And when we cannot sleep...
We fling the windows open wide.
We breathe up and down the avenue...
Howling out our windy insides.

When sleep finally comes...
The wind living inside of me...
Relaxes breathing in and out...
In perfect synchronicity.

GIGGLE

At the most serious times of all...
There's a giggle inside of me.
It bubbles and bubbles inside my tummy...
Until the giggle overpowers me.

"Please! Please!" I beg.
"Don't make me giggle!"
With a giggle, she finally agrees...
Her giggle makes me wriggle!

Wriggling and giggling in assembly...
Are two things which teachers don't
like to see!
"I can't help it!" I explain...
"There's a giggle inside of me!"

SWAN

On the riverbed my friend and I sit side by side...
Watching the swans float by majestically...
I wonder what it would be like to be a swan...
Next thing I know there's one inside of me.

The feathers tickle inside my tummy...
As I say hello to the swan inside of me.
She ruffles her feathers but doesn't answer...
My stomach rumbles and we are both hungry...

We go down to the kitchen; I open the fridge...
But have no idea how to feed the swan in me.
"What do you like to eat?" I ask.
She says, "I can't eat anything I can see!"

"What about bread?" I ask.
I'd heard bread was a favourite swan food...
"It's bad for us," she says...
"But grass is very good."

So, I make myself a sandwich...
And out into the garden go the swan and me.
She feasts on the grass outside - blech!
And I enjoy my peanut butter and jelly.

When we return to the river she thanks me.
I say she is welcome, then look down.
She places something on my head...
In the reflected water I see it is a crown.

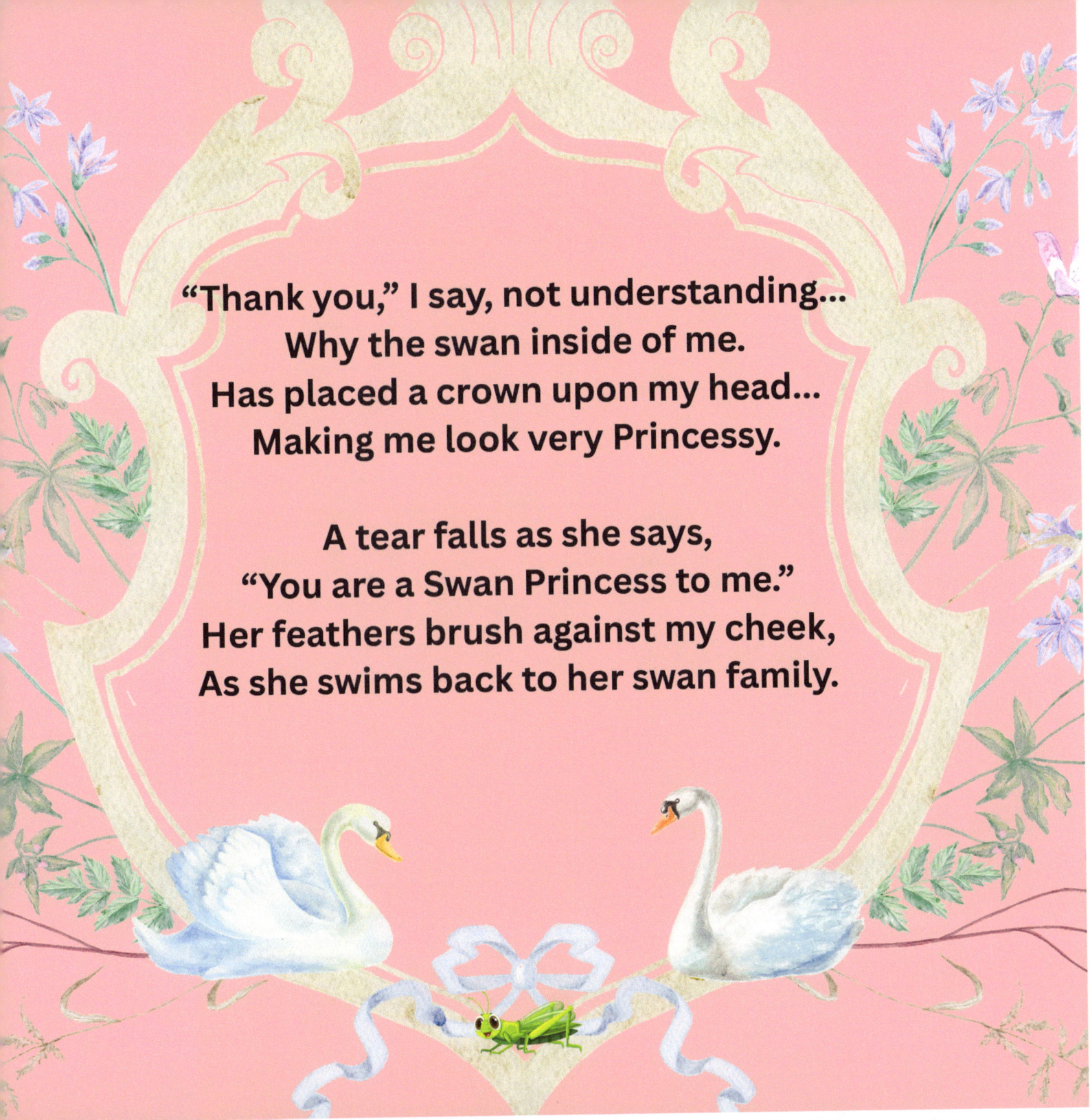

"Thank you," I say, not understanding...
Why the swan inside of me.
Has placed a crown upon my head...
Making me look very Princessy.

A tear falls as she says,
"You are a Swan Princess to me."
Her feathers brush against my cheek,
As she swims back to her swan family.

CERBERUS

Dogs should only have one head!
Unlike the one living inside of me.
He has three big heads!
He is a Cerberus you see!

I prefer it when he is sound asleep.
Then it is like he was never there!
I can pretend he isn't until...
HE has a nightmare!

Then I call out, "Mommy help!"
The Cerberus loves my singing Mommy!
Her voice seems to sooth and calm...
The Cerberus inside of me!

HEDGEHOG

Hedgehogs look prickly!
But not the one inside of me!
When he curls up in a tiny ball...
He lets me tickle his tummy!

SLOTH

"Sleep. Sleep. I need more sleep!"
Says the sloth living inside of me.
I say, "It's easy, just go to sleep then!
And stop waking me!"

The sloth yawns and falls asleep.
I can't sleep now! And I feel grumpy!
Sloths were sure more interesting...
When one wasn't living inside of me!

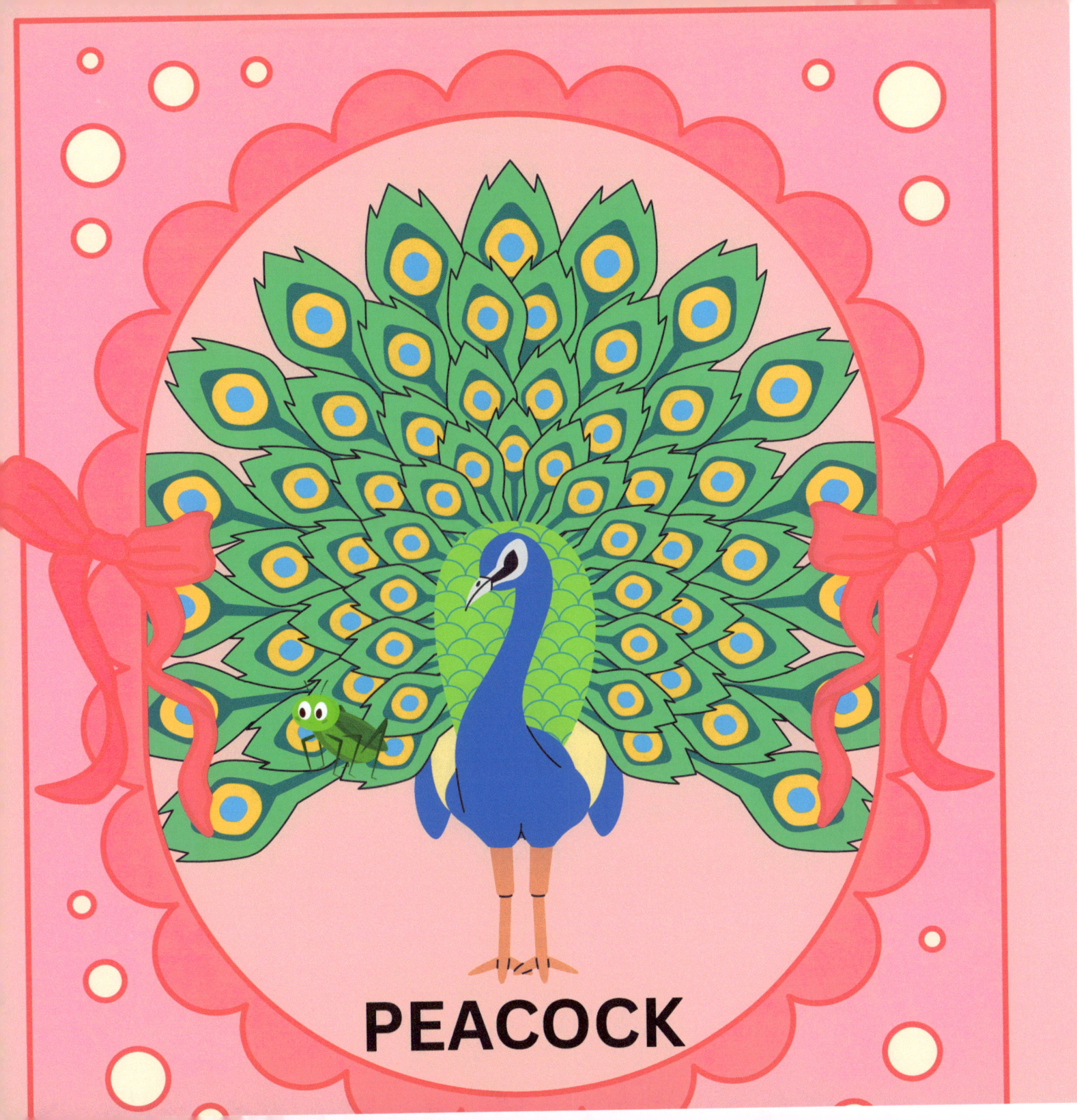

PEACOCK

Why must I be first in line?
Why must I stand out more as me?
Perhaps it is because...
There's a peacock inside of me.

Peacocks, by their very nature...
Attract attention for all to see!
Adorned in feathered royalty
Meant for stardom - JUST LIKE ME!

TERN

Grandpa said, "Did you know there's a song
called *Turn, Turn, Turn*?"
I said, "No. What kind of song might it be?"
He said the words are from the bible...
Next thing I knew there was a tern inside of me!

A tern is a bird similar to a seagull.
The song Grandpa mentioned was by The Byrds...
We sat by the lake fishing...
And Grandpa taught me the words.

We never caught anything on that day...
Because the tern inside of me.
Kept diving into the water and nabbing...
Every single fish it could see!

"Well, that's a tern for the worse!" Grandpa said.
I couldn't help but agree.
"For every season, *Tern, Tern, Tern!*"
Grandpa and I sang joyfully.

PANDA

I have a panda named Amanda,
Living inside of me.
She likes to wear sunglasses at night...
Which seems quite unpanda-like to me.

"Why do you need sunglasses at night?" I ask.
Amanda the panda adjusts her glasses
immediately.
Amanda the panda does not reply...
I offer a suggestion, politely.

"You could wear a silky mask instead," I suggest.
I remove the sunglasses so she can give it a try.
She takes it off and flings it across the room!
And Amanda the panda begins to cry.

"Why are you crying? I ask.
She says the mask was obscene!
Because it blocked out her vision...
I said, "Oh, I see what you mean."

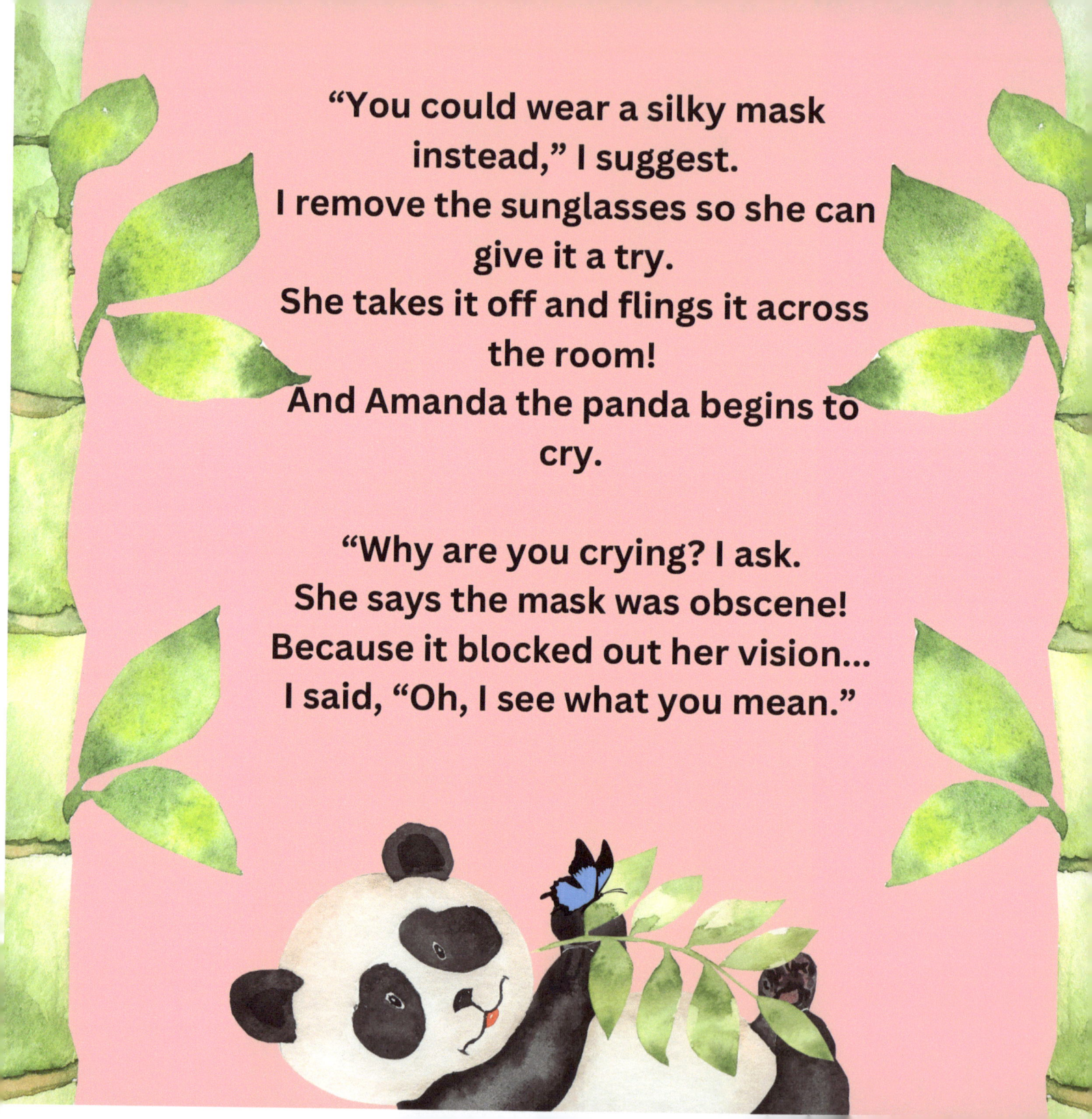

"But you don't need glasses at night," I said.
"I do," she replied, "when you look at your screen."
Now I was the reason for her wearing sunglasses...
By sneaking a peek when I shouldn't have been!

"The glare from the screen hurts my eyes!" she cried.
"It's why I need the sunglasses at night!"
Amanda the panda continued to cry...
Her sobbing gave me quite a fright.

It seemed a compromise was needed...
Soon everything was set to right!
I didn't look at the screen after bedtime...
And Amanda the panda didn't need sunglasses at night!

STAR

Make a Wish

I wonder how many wishes I get...
When there's a star inside of me.
Perhaps as many as one a day?
Maybe even two, or three?

But if I could make a wish every day...
I might run out of things to wish for.
If the star was inside of me...
Wishing might turn into a bore!

make a wish!

So, I think I will stick with one birthday wish a year...
And hold my wishes to myself tightly...
Too much of anything can never be good...
When there is a star living inside of me.

HOME

My family moves around a lot...
But I always know where I'm meant to be.
That's because everywhere we go...
My home lives inside of me.

The sky above me is always blue...
With clouds scattered in between...
The grass always smells sweet and pure...
With lots of flowers and plenty of green.

Welcome Home

Mommy, daddy, granny, and gramps...
Are here, and will always be.
Smiling and singing as always...
In the home inside of me.

KITE

The wind lifts me off the ground!
Up, up, and away I fly!
As the kite inside of me
Takes me high, high, up in the sky.

"Don't look down!" the kite sings,
As its tail is lifted by the wind.
"What's the point in flying, then?" I ask...
He laughs as his tail begins to spin!

Up high is where I am meant to be!
With the kite inside of me.
Even when we need to be rescued...
When the wind blows us into a tree!

CONGA DANCER

I am never alone anymore...
Since a conga line formed inside of me.
Even when it's late and I'm trying to sleep...
Someone always yells, "LET'S PARTY!"

People come out,
The minute the music begins...
We form a conga line
And every dancer wins!

If I was sleepy, I'm not anymore
As I shuffle along to the beat.
I never knew being a conga dancer
Would be such a treat!

PARACHUTE

Sometimes I get restless...
Especially when I have to wear a suit.
Thank goodness inside of me...
Is an adventurous parachute!

The parachute makes me take chances...
Like when I jump on the trampoline at school.
Of course, I always keep safe...
Even when I act like a fool!

I can always rescue myself, you see...
With the parachute inside of me.
An adventure awaits me every day...
Under its multicoloured symphony.

WRITE A POEM

DRAW A PICTURE

ALSO BY CATHY MCGOUGH

<u>POETRY SERIES:</u>

There's a Chimpanzee Inside of Me!
There's a Jumping Bean Inside of Me!
There's a Reindeer Inside of Me!
There's a Hero inside of Me!

<u>JUMP SERIES:</u>

Jump Like a Caribou!
Jump Like a Kangaroo!
Jump at the Zoo!
Jump and Say P.U.!
Jump and Say Boo!
Jump and Say Valentine's Day Is
For Kids Too!
Jump and Look For a Clue!
Jump and Say Happy Birthday to You!
Jump For Everything Blue!
Jump, Hop and Say Happy Easter To You!
Jump and Say Cock-A-Doodle-Do!
Jump and Sing Da-Do-Do-Do!
Jump and Ask Who? Who?
Jump and Squawk Like a Cockatoo!
Jump and Ask Is It You or Ewe?
Jump and Say There's an Ewww in My Stew!
Jump and Say Merry Christmas To You!
Jump and Cheer Happy New Year!
Jump and Say There's a Moo-Moo in a Tutu!
Jump and Say There's a Hare in My Hair!
Jump and Say My Aunt Ate An Ant!
Jump and Say There's An Aardvark
In The Amusement Park!
Jump and Roar For The Dinosaurs!
Jump and Buzz Like A Bee!
Jump and Flutter Like A Butterfly!
Jump and Pop Like Popcorn!
Jump and Ribbit Like A Frog!
Jump and Snore Like A Koala!

Jump and Snuffle Like A Platypus!
Jump and Grunt Like A Groundhog!
Jump and Say Hello!
Jump and Say Friend!
Jump and Say Peace!
Jump and Say Sky!
Jump and Say Merry Christmas!
Jump and Say Happy New Year!
Jump and Say Fun!
Jump and Say Family!
Jump and Say Jump!

<u>CLAP FOR SERIES:</u>

Clap for 1!
Clap for 2!
Clap for 3!
Clap for 4!
Clap for 5!
Clap for 6!
Clap for 7!
Clap for 8!
Clap for 9!
Clap for 10!

The Cat Who Said Hello
The Three Boulders
Billy Shakespeare
Billie Shakespeare
Learn To Draw With Symmetry
ABC More Learn to Draw With Symmetry

<u>Non-Fiction</u>
103 Fundraising Ideas For Parent Volunteers With Schools and Teams